Daisy went out for her special
birthday dessert.

"I'd like three scoops of
ice cream with extra fudge,"
Daisy said.

2

Daisy's dessert wasn't just
big. It was enormous!

Daisy began to gobble up the dessert. She ate and ate. The dessert grew smaller. Her tummy grew bigger.

4

Daisy didn't stop until every
last bit of ice cream was gone.
She even licked the spoon.

Then it was time to go home.
Daisy rolled off her chair. She
rolled across the room and out
onto the sidewalk.

6

Daisy was too full to move.
Her parents had to roll her home.

"Maybe I shouldn't have
had that last bite," Daisy said.